To Mic...
Happy Birthday
love Tiffany
xx

Before the Dinosaurs

A Cherrytree Book

Designed and produced by
A S Publishing

First published 1988
by Cherrytree Press Ltd
a subsidiary of
The Chivers Company Ltd
Windsor Bridge Road
Bath, Avon BA2 3AX

Copyright © Cherrytree Press Ltd 1988

British Library Cataloguing in Publication Data

Head, John G.
  Before the dinosaurs.—(The Ages of Earth)
  1. Prehistoric organisms – For childen
  I. Title II. Robinson, Bernard, *1930-*
  III. Series
  560

  ISBN 0-7451-5012-8

Printed in Hong Kong by Colorcraft Ltd

All rights reserved. No part of this publication may be reproduced, stored in a retrieval system, or transmitted, in any form or by any means without the prior permission in writing of the publiser, nor be otherwise circulated in any form of binding or cover other than that in which it is published and without a similar condition including this condition being imposed on the subequent purchaser.

THE AGES OF EARTH

Before the Dinosaurs

By John G. Head
Illustrated by Bernard Robinson

CHERRYTREE BOOKS

Everyone slept deeply as the Time Shuttle sped soundlessly on in time. When they landed, it would be late in the Devonian Period, about 360 million years ago.

Mike had won a prehistoric world tour for two in a competition. His sister Helen had not really wanted to come; she felt she was a bit old for dinosaurs. In fact they had not seen a dinosaur yet but they had come across other strange and terrifying creatures.

The expedition was captained by Bob Marsh, with Lieutenant 'Atty' Atkins as his second in command. Jen Andrews was their Space-Time ranger. She knew almost as much about the prehistoric world as Timcom, the on-board computer – and she was a lot more fun.

lobe-finned fish
(Eusthenopteron)

So far, they had only seen sea creatures, because the earliest living things lived only in the water. The land was mostly bare and lifeless. Mike wanted to be the first to spot a proper land animal – an amphibian. He thought he had seen one as they took off the day before.

'That fish thing we saw on the shore as we were taking off, Timcom, what was it?' asked Mike after breakfast.
'That was Eusthenopteron, a lobe-finned fish that could live out of water,' said Timcom, putting a picture of it on to the screen.
'Why would a fish want to live out of water?' said Helen. 'It seems silly to me.'

'Well, with so many other creatures in the water, it might have been able to get more food on land,' said Timcom.

'But how could it move and breathe?' asked Mike. 'Fish have no legs and no lungs. They die out of water.'

'That's true of most fish,' said Timcom. 'But even in our own time there are some fish that can survive for a time in dried-up ponds. They have evolved lungs as well as gills. They can also move about on their fins.

'A full-grown Eusthenopteron could probably not support its weight on land. But its young might, and on land they would be safe from all the big fish trying to eat them. So that's another reason for a fish to move on to the land.'

'We are about to land ourselves,' said Jen.

'Still not many plants,' said Helen as the Shuttle touched down. 'The hills are all bare.'

'There are lots more than there were,' said Jen. 'I can't wait to go and have a look at all that greenery by the stream, and see if there are any amphibians.'

'You'll have to wear life-support suits again,' said Captain Marsh, 'just in case the air is not pure enough for you to breathe. And don't be too long. This is only a short stop. We've a lot more to do today.'

Jen, Mike and Helen climbed into their space-suits and set off along the course of the nearby stream. The water was full of fish and, for the first time, there were creepy crawlies on the ground, and plants with stems.

They had walked over a mile when Jen let out a cry of delight, which the others heard over the intercom. 'Look,' she said, 'spawn.'

In the water there was a clump of black-spotted jelly, just like frogspawn only bigger. There were also some things like newt tadpoles, with frilly gills on their heads.

'Whatever laid those eggs must be around somewhere. Go carefully, we don't want to frighten it,' said Jen.

'Can you sense where it is, Timcom?' she asked the all-knowing computer.

'No, but I can tell you that the spawn belongs to Ichthyostega, the first amphibian we know about. You'd best find a sheltered place near the water. That's where it will be.'

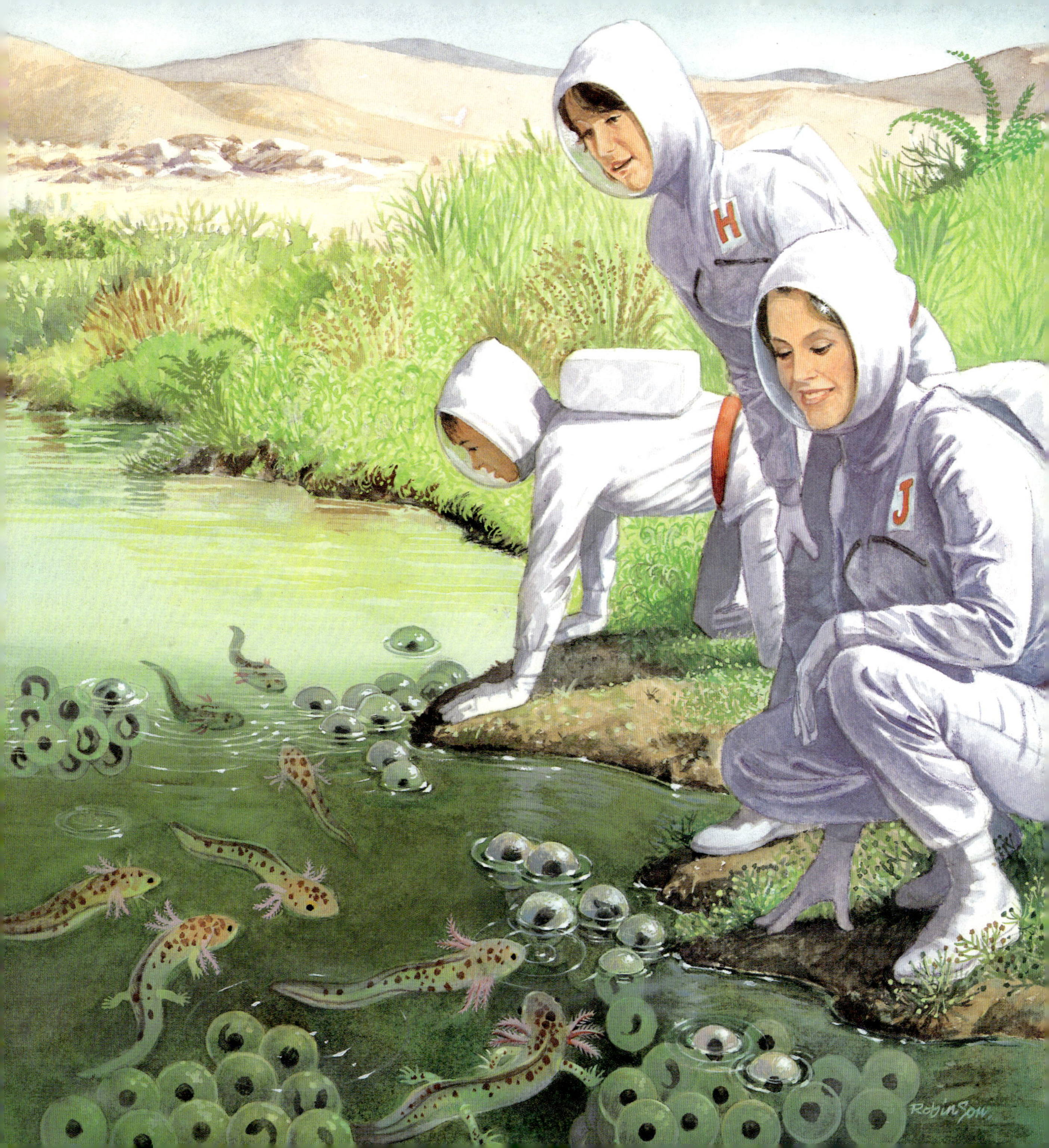
H
J
Robinson

And that's where they found it, just crawling out from under a rock. It was green and spotty and about a metre long. They watched the creature until Timcom said it was time to go back. As they walked, Jen instructed Timcom to photograph certain plants. She explained to the others that nobody knew much about early prehistoric plants; they were too fragile to have fossilized easily.

Helen and Mike were not terribly interested in the plants. They wanted their lunch and hurried on ahead. Suddenly they stopped. 'What on earth is that?' shrieked Mike.

Ichthyostega

Across their path crawled a millipede that seemed to go on for ever. It was huge.

'It's like an endless train. Look at all its legs,' said Jen, catching them up. 'It must be two metres long.'

'One of the larger millipedes,' said Timcom. 'Its ancestors probably left the water before the fish. Their bodies didn't have to adapt much for life on land, and they eat plants so there is plenty of food for them.'

'It would make a lovely lunch for us all,' said Mike.

'Ugh,' said Jen. 'All right for an amphibian like Ichthyostega, but not for me.'

millipede

Ichthyostega

After they had had lunch, squeezed out from a tube as usual, they got ready to move on to the Carboniferous Period, a short hop of 20 million years. Now that there was life on land, they had to make sure that they didn't accidentally take any insects or larger creatures with them, for fear of upsetting the balance of nature.

Once they had checked the Shuttle, they took off into Earth orbit and then went into time mode. As usual everything went eerily black outside. Jen and Helen took up their books and Mike had a few words with Timcom.

'Was Ichthyostega the first land animal?' he asked.
'No,' said the computer. 'That millipede's ancestors

probably lived on land long before amphibians evolved. The first land creatures had to rely on plants for food. Amphibians don't eat plants, so they couldn't have evolved until there were enough other creatures for them to eat. It took millions of years.

'Ichthyostega lived on land, but it had to go back to the water to lay its eggs, and it was tied to the water anyway because of its skin.'

'What was wrong with its skin?' asked Mike, peering at the picture on the screen.

'It wasn't waterproof,' said Timcom. 'Land animals need waterproof skins to stop their bodies drying out. That's why you only find amphibians in damp places.'

They all got a surprise when they came in to land in the Carboniferous Period. Everywhere was green, with vast forests and swamps. It was hard to find a place to land.

'Be careful when you go out,' said Captain Marsh, 'the land is often very swampy. Stick to the rocks or places where there are tall trees growing. Wear your lesion-proof undersuits in case you get bitten. There's no need for life-support suits any more. Timcom has tested the air, and it's fine.'

'I think I might stay here and finish my book,' said Helen. She didn't like the sound of being bitten.

'Come on, Helen,' said Mike. 'It won't be any fun without you and I need you to hold my hand.'

'Look at the plants,' said Jen, as they walked along. 'We'll get Timcom to tell us about them – when we get back,' she added, to stop Timcom launching into a speech.

It was difficult to avoid looking at the plants. Some of them were thirty metres tall, and they were so thick the sun could only just penetrate them. In the eerie half-light they could hear insects buzzing and water lapping.

Pushing their way towards the light they came to a clear pool, full of long, thin, writhing creatures.

'Snakes!' said Mike.

'No,' said Timcom, through the intercom. 'More amphibians. Snakes are reptiles, creatures that evolved from amphibians. You won't see reptiles yet.'

giant clubmosses
giant horsetails
Cordaites
tree fern
lepospondyls

They watched the creatures for a while and then made their way round the pond. A huge dragonfly skimmed across the surface. It was beautiful but scary.

The ground by the pond was a bit soft, so they headed back to the higher, firmer ground. The air was thick with insects that pinged against the visors of their helmets. Thank heaven for the helmets, thought Helen.

Suddenly Mike screamed again. This time he had been the first to spot a giant scorpion. It was just by Helen's hand, and the poisonous sting in its tail glistened.

giant mayfly

giant dragonfly

'I don't like this,' said Helen, and took to her heels. She ran as fast as she could but the dense undergrowth made speed impossible. She looked back and saw Jen and Mike examining the scorpion as though it were a kitten. As she did so, she tripped and fell into the undergrowth.

The fronds of a huge fern closed over her. She scrambled to her feet and tried to push the plants away. Ahead of her there was a clear patch of ground; if only she could reach it. She stumbled on and suddenly felt something hit her helmet. She put her hand up to move what she took to be a plant stem. But it wasn't. It was a thread of silk.

giant scorpion

Looking up Helen saw that she had stumbled into the lair of a huge, hairy spider. The spider had come out to see what it had caught. Helen backed away, and screamed. She had always been scared of spiders and this one was almost a metre wide.

Frozen to the spot, she screamed again. Jen and Mike were miles away. There was nothing she could do but scream. She had forgotten that Timcom could hear her. The computer had, of course, sounded the alarm immediately, located her and sent Bob and Atty to help her.

They arrived to find her still rooted to the spot. Jen and Mike, having heard the excitement, had hurried to find her as well.

'Gosh,' said Mike. 'What a beauty!' and he and Jen set about examining the spider and getting its vital statistics from Timcom.

'I think it's time we gave up for today,' said Bob. 'It's getting dark and I don't suppose you'd like to spend the night in the forest, would you?'

'But we haven't seen everything,' pleaded Mike.

'I've seen quite enough,' said Helen.

'Well, you can stay out for a bit longer, but stay together. Helen should not have been left on her own.'

'Well, I wasn't quite alone was I?' said Helen. 'Thanks for saving me, Timcom.'

'You didn't need saving,' said Timcom. 'Spiders don't eat people, and even the scorpion couldn't pierce your suit.'

giant spider

After supper, Jen, Bob and Helen played cards. Atty input the log and Mike, as usual, asked Timcom about all the things they had seen.

Next morning he told everyone about the plants and trees they had seen – giant ferns, horsetails and clubmosses. Atty put the Shuttle into hover mode and took them on an early-morning tour of the forest. Much of the land was flooded; trees were uprooted and lying half-submerged.

   'What's happening?' Mike asked Timcom.
   'What you are looking at is a coal swamp,' said Timcom. 'The trees that fall gradually sink into the mud and decay. Eventually they will turn into —'

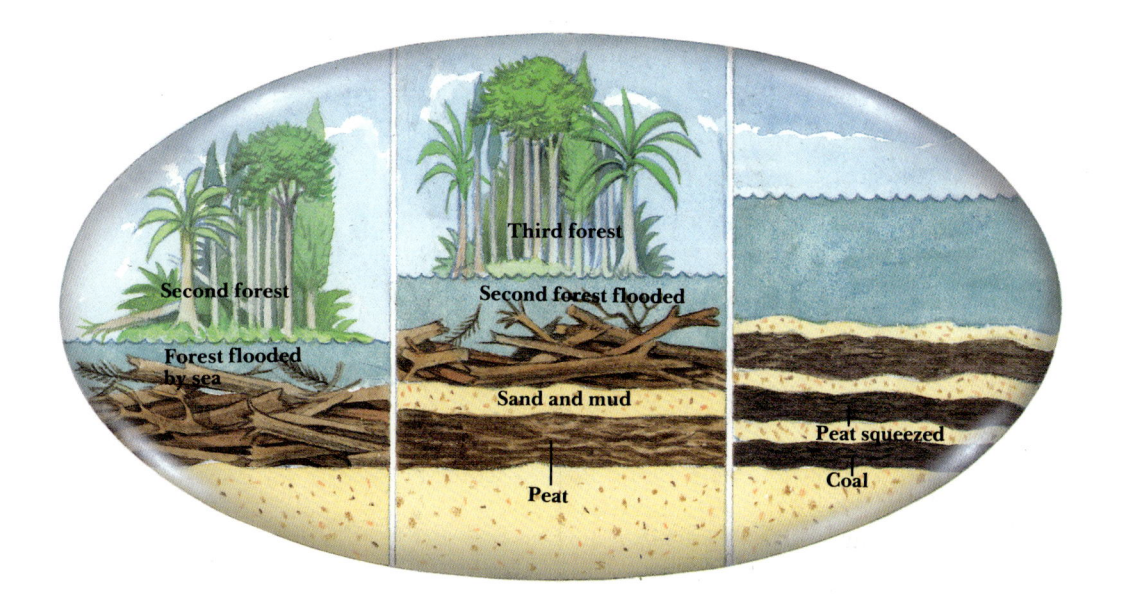

'Coal,' interrupted Helen. She had done coal at school and liked to show Mike that she knew a thing or two.

'How do they turn into coal?' asked Mike. Helen left the explaining to Timcom.

'Millions and millions of trees like these died during Carboniferous times when the land was flooded,' said the computer. 'Their remains built up in thick layers and formed peat. New plants grew on top of the peat. Then, maybe thousands of years later, the sea flooded the land again and dumped mud and sand on top of the peat. This heavy weight squeezed the peat until it was almost rock hard – in fact, until it became coal. The coal people burn today is the remains of all those giant trees.'

'Think of that,' said Jen, 'when you see coal burning. It was all alive once. Even Helen's spider is now coal.'

After they had looked at the surface for a while, they found a large area of land that had not been flooded. The plants were flourishing and the sun was high. Jen and Mike were eager to go out and explore, but it took half an hour to persuade Helen to venture outside again; and even then she would only go with a stun gun to protect herself.

They stuck to the high ground, but there was not much to see, so they edged their way down to the shore of a lake and watched the dragonflies. Then they noticed a huge animal on the bank opposite. The creature heaved its way over the ground and slid into the water to catch a fish. This must be a reptile, thought Mike, it's at least five metres long, and it looks like a crocodile.

But it wasn't a reptile, it was another amphibian called Eogyrinus.

Jen was really keen to see a reptile. Reptiles first lived in Carboniferous times, but not many fossils of them have been found. She would have loved to have found a living one to film, or even some reptile eggs.

They watched Eogyrinus for a while and then Mike noticed another smaller creature.
   'That could be a reptile,' he said. 'It's small enough.'
   'Where?' asked Jen, stepping towards the fallen tree that Mike was pointing at. The little animal was sheltering under it.
   'It's there,' he said, 'right at the end.'

Eogyrinus

Jen edged along the trunk, leaning over to try to glimpse the animal. But the trunk would not bear her weight. It tipped up and sank into the swampy edge of the lake. Jen toppled after it and began to sink.

Mike ran towards her but Helen screamed to him to stop. 'Throw something she can hang on to, there's no point falling in yourself.'

There was a tree fern bending over the swamp. It bent even more under Mike's weight as he climbed along it, but still he could not reach Jen who was up to her chest in the mud.
    'Hold on Jen,' he yelled, and shinned down the tree and took

Microbrachis
(an amphibian)

off his suit. Then he climbed the tree again and tied the arms of his suit round the trunk so that Jen was able to catch hold of the legs. But she still could not move. She was safe only so long as the suit and the tree would hold.

'Stay there. I'm going for the others,' said Helen. 'Timcom obviously can't hear what's happened.'

Helen rushed headlong back the way they had come, leaping over plants and brushing aside the insects and spiders in her path. Twice she fell and picked herself up. She must find Bob and Atty. Suppose they were not there. Suppose the Shuttle wasn't there. Timcom wasn't working, so anything could have happened.

Helen ran on and on, imagining all the worst things that could happen. Then a dreadful thing did happen; a huge armoured animal was blocking her path. It was too big to leap over or get round. It had come out from under an overhanging rock to eat the leaf litter. Its chomping jaws were making a dreadful noise. She threw a piece of rock at the creature but it would not shift. She had dropped her stun gun long before. There was nothing for it; she would have to climb over it.

She walked gingerly towards it and suddenly it saw her. She froze; but instead of spitting poison at her as she feared it might, it moved slowly back under the ledge.

arthropleurid

Helen could still see it as she edged past. It made her feel quite sick. But the thought of Mike and Jen kept her going. She hurtled towards the Shuttle, and there at last were Bob and Atty hurrying towards her with a rope.

'Of course Timcom did not pack up,' said Bob. 'It transmitted an alarm as soon as Jen fell and we had Timcom's pictures. None of you thought to say what had happened.'

'We were too busy,' said Helen. 'Come on, let's hurry. Mind that great big thing there,' she said, as they came up to the creature.

Was this the same Helen who had met the spider the previous day? Bob and Atty could not believe their ears!

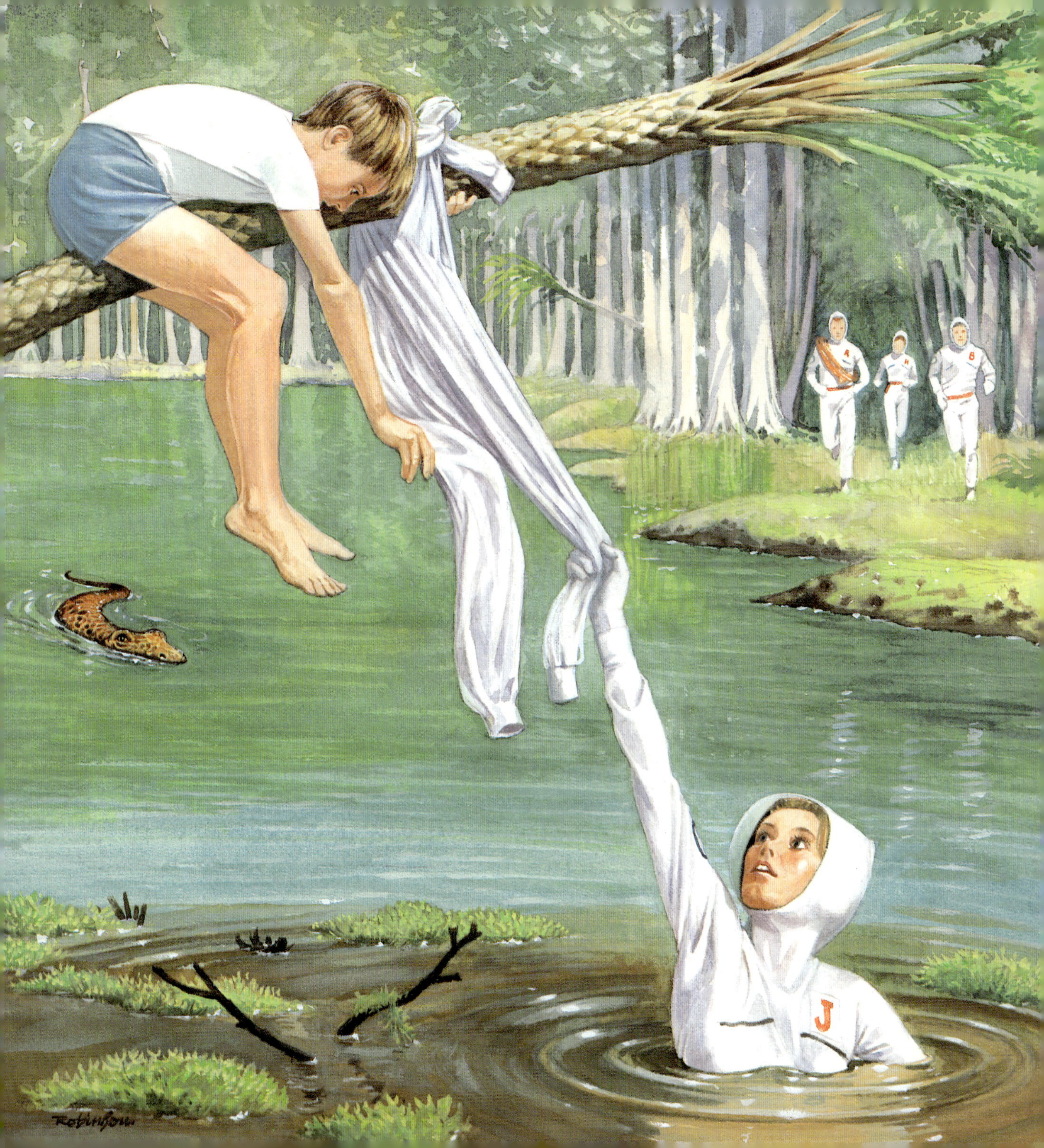
Robinson

Soon they reached the swamp. Jen was still hanging on for dear life and Mike was still holding down the tree. Both of them were waiting for the terrible ripping sound of its roots being torn out of the ground. It seemed to them ages since Helen had gone. In reality it was only minutes. Jen had bravely been explaining to Mike that the little creature was not a reptile but an amphibian called Microbrachis.
 'It's my fault,' she said. 'I should have known that a reptile would not have been hiding from the sun. They love the warmth!'

Atty and Bob threw Jen the rope and pulled her out.
 'You are a fine one to be a ranger,' said Bob, hugging Jen. 'You are supposed to stop the others doing foolish things.'

Helen helped Mike down from the tree and they all headed back to the Shuttle. Suddenly Mike screamed,
 'Look at that!' and pointed at the creature who was once more blocking their path. It was, according to Jen, who was as enthusiastic as ever despite her ordeal, an arthropleurid – an extinct creepy crawly that lived on the forest floor.
 'Oh, don't mind that old thing,' said Helen, as they crept past. 'It won't hurt you.'

THE AGES OF EARTH TOUR

Shuttle back in time and see with your own eyes 600 million years of Earth's history in just three weeks.

Periods	Years Ago (Millions)	Plants and Animals
Pre-cambrian Time	4500	No life on Earth to start with. Tiny plants appear about 3000 million years ago in the sea; first known animals appear about 700 million years ago.
Cambrian	600	No life on land, but in the sea there are creatures called graptolites and trilobites, corals and sponges, shellfish and jellyfish.
Ordovician	500	More graptolites and trilobites in sea. Creatures called brachiopods and the first fish – which have armour.
Silurian	440	Land plants appear. Lots of fish in the sea and giant sea-scorpions.
Devonian	395	The age of fishes. Sea teems with all kinds, including huge jawed fish and sharks. Small creatures leave the sea to live on land. Amphibians evolve from fish.
Carboniferous	345	Giant land plants in coal swamps. Large amphibians and the first insects, including some giants. Reptiles evolve from amphibians.
Permian	280	Lots more reptiles and fewer amphibians. Trilobites die out.

PALAEOZOIC ERA (Cambrian through Permian)

THE AGES OF EARTH TOUR

Visit each of these periods and see the animals and plants of bygone ages, monsters of land and sea and sky.

	Periods	Years Ago (Millions)	Plants and Animals
MESOZOIC ERA	Triassic	225	The first dinosaurs. Large reptiles and shelled creatures called ammonites in the sea. Mammals evolve from reptiles.
	Jurassic	200	Lots of dinosaurs, including huge sauropods and carnosaurs. Pterosaurs in the air. Birds evolve from reptiles.
	Cretaceous	135	New kinds of dinosaurs, including ones with armour. Small mammals and birds. First flowering plants. At the end of the period dinosaurs and many other creatures die out.
CENOZOIC ERA	Tertiary	65	The age of mammals. Many kinds of mammals evolve, including horses, elephants and apes. Coniferous forests and grasslands.
	Quaternary	2	Mammoths, woolly rhinos and sabre-toothed cats live through Ice Ages. Ancestors of humans evolve from apes. The first humans appear.

Index

Ammonites 31
Amphibians 6, 8, 11, 14, 29, 30
Animals, evolution of 6, 7, 13, 14, 30, 31
Apes 31
Armoured fish 30
Arthropleurid 27, 29
Arthropod 29

Birds 31

Cambrian Period 30
Carboniferous Period 12, 14, 21, 23, 30
Carnosaurs 31
Cenozoic Era 31
Clubmosses, giant 15, 20
Coal 21
Coal swamp 20, 21, 30
Coniferous forests 31
Corals 30
Cordaites 15
Cretaceous Period 31

Devonian Period 5
Dinosaurs 5, 31
Dragonflies, giant 16, 17, 22

Earth, history of 30, 31
Elephants 31
Eogyrinus 23
Eusthenopteron 6, 7
Evolution 6, 7, 13, 14, 30, 31

Fern, giant 15, 20
Fish 6, 7, 30

Graptolites 30
Grassland 31

Horses 31
Horsetails, giant 15, 20
Humans, ancestors of 31

Ice Ages 31
Ichthyostega 8-10, 12, 13
Insects 14, 30

Jawed fish 30
Jellyfish 30
Jurassic Period 31

Lepospondyls 15
Lobe-finned fish 15

Mammals 31
Mammoths 31
Mayfly 17
Mesozoic Era 31
Microbrachis 24, 29
Millipede, giant 11, 12

Ordovician Period 30

Palaeozoic Era 30
Peat 21
Permian Period 30
Plants 8, 10, 14, 15, 20, 21, 30, 31
Pre-cambrian times 30
Pterosaurs 31

Quaternary Period 31

Reptiles 23, 30, 31

Sabre-toothed cats 31
Sauropods 31
Scorpion, giant 16-18
Sea-scorpions 30
Sharks 30
Shellfish 30
Silurian Period 30
Spawn 8
Spider, giant 18, 19, 21, 27
Sponges 30
Swamp 20-25, 29

Tertiary Period 31
Trees 14, 15, 20, 21
Triassic Period 31
Trilobites 30

Woolly rhinos 31